Love Poured Out

POETRY BY DELORES HANSEN ALCORN

HARPSTRING BOOKS
An imprint of
WRITTEN WORLD COMMUNICATIONS

Love Poured Out

©2013 by Delores Hansen Alcorn
Published by Harpstring Books,
an Imprint of Written World Communications
PO Box 26677
Colorado Springs, CO 80936
Written-World.com

Brought to you by the creative team at Written-World.com:
Lynda K. Arndt, Dale R. Hansen, and Kristine Pratt
Front cover design by Lynda K. Arndt

Interior Photography by Lynda K. Arndt and others found on Wikimedia Commons, used by right of the Creative Commons License, and credited as follows:

> Pacific Ocean, Vinyard, and Old Books by Brocken Inaglory
> Pottery by Norbert Nagel
> Smile by D. Sharon Pruitt from Hill Air Force Base, Utah, USA
> City by Mark Ryan
> Cirrus Cloud by Przemyslaw "BlueShade" Idzkiewicz
> Cross by Chris Dodd
> Tree in Bryce Canyon by Caaz
> Chaplain by Photographer's Mate 2nd Class Eric Powell
> Grief by Bernd Ruchhoeft
> Hands by Petar Milošević
> Cocoon by Gwillhickers
> Salt of the Earth by רזע הנח
> Old books by William Hoiles from Basking Ridge, NJ, USA

Library of Congress Control Number: 2012956224
International Standard Book Number: 978-1-938679-03-2

Printed in the United States of America

My Prayer

Little Book, be on your way
May God bless what you have to say
I pray you'll prick the heart of sinners
And strengthen all the new beginners
Tune the nerves of every saint
With song and love and prayer acquaint

Stepping Stones

One step at a time is all He asks
He will give strength for all my tasks
Jesus says, Leave the next step to Me
For I will never fail Thee

I do not know what lies ahead
But He goes before as He has said
I grieve, my Lord, when I am sad
If I but trust, He'll make me glad

Thus Saith the Lord

Unto you, who choose the things that are pleasing before me
I will give a place in My dwelling
That will last for eternity

Unto you, who take hold of My covenant
I will lead you forth with peace
And I will give to you a name that shall never cease

My thoughts are not your thoughts, nor are you ways Mine
As the heavens are higher than the earth
So much higher is the Divine

Ho, everyone that thirsteth, come to the water and drink
I will give you so much more than you could ask or think

Unto him who has no money, I say come and buy
For in all My holy mountain, no need shall pass you by

This everlasting covenant I do make with you
You shall feast with Me in glory
Your joys forever new

I lay your foundations with sapphires, and many a colored stone
My peace upon My children
My glory shall be known

Upon this holy mountain, the trees do clap with glee
Take hold of My covenant, My people
For I give this unto thee

Call to Repentance

May I just remind you
That within you is a soul?
Christ waits to dwell within you
Just let Him have control

Then He will lift the load you carry
And lovingly guide your way
If we but with Him tarry
His grace is sufficient for the day

But if you do not heed His calling
You will perish in eternal Hell
Though this may seem appalling
It is what His Word does tell

I pray you will come to the Savior now
You will find that God is good
And excuses are not valid somehow
When His Word is understood

God, Our Maker

Where is God, our Maker
        Who gives a song in the night?
Where is God, our Maker
        Who gives His creatures sight
And gives to man more wisdom
        Than to animals or birds that fly?
Will He hear and answer
        When unto Him I cry?
Oh, yes! He carefully watches
        The whole of all mankind
No darkness ever is thick enough
        For one to hide behind
His eye is on the sparrow
        And He carefully watches all
He knows the ones who seek Him
        As He knows all those who fall
He brings about all justice
        Upon Him I will wait!
I must show His love to others
        Before it is too late
His love is deeper than the ocean
        And higher than the stars
All men will fall before Him
        When he clears away the bars

Broken Vessel

Just an earthen vessel, cracked and worn
But in His image, I am reborn
This old vessel must be broken indeed
So I may know another's need
For even Jesus did bleed and die
Just to free such sinners as you and I
Could I but ask my Lord for more
Than to lead a lamb to Heaven's door?
Lord, I but ask Thy will be done
That I spill your love to touch someone
You are the Potter, I am the clay
Remake this vessel with love and care
For I cannot sorrow when Jesus is there

Hath not the potter power over the clay,
of the same lump to make one vessel unto honour,
and another unto dishonour?
Romans 9:21 (KJV)

The Angel's Call

I saw a city in the midnight hour
Its lights all shining from street and tower
But all around, darkness is falling
Does anyone hear the angel calling?

The city sleeps; its lights all glisten
How many are there who care to listen?
The angel warns with a trumpet voice
But some only hear the city's noise

Love's Arrow

Does the arrow through the heart cause love
Could it fly in like a gentle dove
It goes in one way and out the other
To open my heart for another

Is this what true love is all about
What goes in must then come out
It goes beyond the piercing pain
Without the arrow could I ever gain

God sends His arrow to the heart
He does not want man from Him to part
He aims His arrow from above
That we may give Him back our love

He wants to pierce the heart of stone
For He sees me from His holy throne
He took sin's arrow to the cross
Into the heart for sins great loss

Sin pulled the arrow out of God's son
As He bled and died for everyone
To save us all from evil's Sheol
For God is a lover of every soul

To deeply love will cause us pain
But perfect love will stand the strain
For God in His mercy lifts it up
That we may drink salvation's cup

The only to stop His arrow is sin
And He does not force His arrows in
The arrow of His love will pierce my heart's core
That He may pour in His love or evermore

Who Am I?

I walked along a dusty road
I carried such a heavy load
I could not see the sun for dust
I knew no one that I could trust

I rested on a grassy slope
I thought with life I could not cope
I gazed out on the lake so still
I sought the Lord my lack to fill

I did not know I could not see
I must have Christ to set me free
I cried, O Lord, I know You care!
I bowed my head in silent prayer

I felt His presence flood my soul
I knew then heaven was my goal
I then began to journey on
I realized my load was gone

I blessed the dust beneath my feet
I heard the songs of birds so sweet
I saw the sun behind the cloud
I began to praise Him long and loud

Fallow Ground

In Jesus I'm secure and strong
His holy word is life and song
I have no need to live in fear
Nor try another's sin to cure

If I but let my shepherd lead the way
He will give me His perfect words to say
I'll not drop His seeds on fallow ground
Nor keep His living waters bound

I first must work the weed choked soil
That His spirit may clean away the spoil
The sun rays keep the cold earth warm
To protect the seed from evil's harm

If I should plant the seeds on my own
How could they then become fully grown
I must seek the One who holds the seed
Before I plant for another's need

The seeds of the spirit I must use
And His living water I must choose
To let God's spirit fill my need
That I may bear fruit for others to feed

Smile

Come on smile, God loves you
Is a happy face something new
You soon will find the gloom is gone
Even if your smile is pasted on

Are you entangled with you plight
And it seems nothing ever comes out right
Could it add some joy to your fears
If you could smile through your tears

Put on a smile because it grows
It could warm another to the toes
Please do not wear a grumpy frown
It can only serve to pull you down

Smile, you are on God's camera, smile
Stop a moment and stretch awhile
There's no comfort in a grumpy face
And who can wear it in God's grace

☺

Whirlwinds

I have a measure of My Spirit
in every child there
Each a tiny whirlwind
traveling round the square
And as you join with others
you will see it grow
The more united my people
the more My work will go

Now all these tiny whirlwinds
can make a cyclone's strength
Then who can know the height of it
and who can know its length
So as united whirlwinds
we will see great power
Come together, My people,
and I'll strengthen you this hour

With my Spirit united,
you will see My work be done
For all my glorious promises
have really just begun
So come together, My people,
and blow the trumpet loud
All the glory of my grace
is just behind the cloud

The Garden Gate

Come to the garden your needs to fill
The gate is open to all who will
Come to God's Eden without delay
Narrow is the path that leads the way

For all must come by way of the cross
Jesus paid way for sin's great loss
He's calling now, come live within
To be washed in the blood, free of sin

With salvation's pass you may enter here
Come into His garden without fear
If you but listen for the Savior's voice
And it is for you to make the choice

His cross is a bridge over death's abyss
Will you answer as a child of His?
He then will lead you through the dark of night
Into the glory of His holy light

Come into His garden before it is too late
When the sheep are in, He will close the gate
To enter or not, all must choose today
Jesus is calling—He is the way

The Beautiful Shore

I cry like a river and no one hears
I find no comfort to dry my tears
Until I see Your beautiful harbor light
Here is my beacon of hope in the darkest of night

When life seems to lift me up and let me down
I will follow Your beacon to higher ground
In Your light I will reach that beautiful shore
For these troubled waters will rage no more

Lord You know the restless waves in me
And I know that You can calm the sea
Oh how I need your peace be still
Help me to see You my needs to fill

When stormy waters seems all I see
Help me to keep my eyes on Thee
That I may find Your solid ground
For You alone can keep the waters down

Master of All

Lord give me patience this I pray,
As I wait on You to lead the way
What You ask of me I want to do,
And I know that you will help me through

You are the Master, You are the Way
Help me to trust, come what may
You are my Father, I am Your child,
Keep me pure and undefiled

Your are my Creator, my needs You fill
And I know all things pure are Your will
Your are the healer, You are divine
Please touch this frail body of mine

From the deep ocean to the rising sun
Where ever I look I see what You have done
From the meadow of flowers to the mountains of rock
Every tree, of Your glory, talks

When I feel anxious for what lies ahead
Help me to seek Your peace instead
For You are my Father, full of Love
Help me set my eyes on things above

Angels

Today I saw an Angel, still she had no wings
But I thought an angel always flies and sings
She came and walked with me and never said one word
Yet a voice of comfort is what I truly heard

It may have been my friend who and angel told to call
But it must have been an angel to keep me from a fall
Who knew I was in need of a very special friend
To lift me in my spirit more on Jesus to depend

Could I be as an angel to one who has a need
That in the love of Jesus others I could feed
Anyone could be an angel in a friend's disguise
So my angel may be my dearest friend in my thankful eyes

Peace in the Valley

I hear the whippoorwill singing on the old grey shed
Keeping perfect time with its little head
He starts at sunset and stops at dawn
With the morning light he will be gone

His beautiful song brings peace to the night
A creature of dark, he sleeps in the light
I love the deep Valley, dark and still
Where I hear the song of the Whippoorwill

Its call brings such great joy to me
And memories of those who used to be
The crickets join in the chorus I hear
And the night owl is hooting loud and clear

Close bubbles a clear cold spring
It bubbles in tune as night creatures sing
The springs also gently runs on its way
Giving life to the river where children play

Its melody carries until break of dawn
When the creatures of night will all be gone
Giving over to creatures who need the light
For a nighttime of peace and a day of delight

The Holy City

I am just a weary traveler on the road of life
And I'm heading for that city where there is no sin or strife
Oh I can see that Holy City
In the very distance now
It is glowing like a diamond as before Him I will bow
Lord I get so anxious
As I walk this troubled globe
I need Your love and patience until You lift my load
I need Your love and wisdom for all who jostle me
And I need Your Holy Spirit to set another free
At times I find a detour that seems to block my way
But there I find a soul who needs Your love today
Oh I see that Holy City
Around the throne of God
It flashes like the lightening
Its holy righteous rod
Oh I'm heading for that City
Glowing like the sun
And the rainbow of His promise
Surrounds the Holy One
I'm but a weary traveler
And I must keep my eyes on Thee
Until I reach that Holy City
The glory of God's presence I can plainly see

Himself

Of His royal priesthood, He stripped

— Himself

To become our Mediator, He gave

— Himself

On the cross He yielded

— Himself

He claims a people for

— Himself

His Holy Spirit lives within the Comforter
Quicker than the eye He shall return

— Himself

The Son

— Himself

The Father, Son, and Holy Spirit
The Triune God

— Himself

Love Poured Out

Love poured out from heaven above
As Jesus emptied Him of all but love
He was forsaken, I am never alone
For He never forsakes one of His own

Despised and rejected His purpose was won
He was Jesus as man, God's own Son
He went to the grave to overcome death
And renew the Spirit of God's holy breath

Though for now my eyes are dim
He conquered the grave that I may rise with Him
He reached down from heaven to lift me up
It was for me he drank that bitter cup

He was stripped of His cloak to cover me
That my cloak of sin could no longer be
No filth of sin spoiled the garment of His
I am now an heir of His own righteousness

He walked on earth, and with mankind did eat
And gave up His life my sins to delete
He waits now in heaven to welcome His own
And sent here His spirit so I'm never alone

Infirmity

If I get caught up in my busy day
And forget to read the Word and pray
May Thy Spirit help my infirmity
For I long to fellowship with Thee

I would walk in Your garden, in the pure, fresh air
All the burdens and joy, with You to share
I long to fellowship with Thee
Lord, please help my infirmity

I am strong in Your spirit, but my flesh is weak
In all that I do, You will I seek
For I desire to sup with Thee
Heal my flesh of its infirmity

Touch my body, soul and mind
Keep me gentle, sweet and kind
That I may become more like Thee
Dear Lord, heal my infirmity

Little Flower

God gave each little flower its face. His children are as flowers in His field, upon the hills, or among the brush and thorns. When one looks for flowers he does not mind the thorns and brambles. But if you search not for flowers you see only thorns and weeds.

Do flowers worry about the towering, overpowering, weeds and thorns? No, these little ones only come out and smile in their fragrance and beauty, until the place set for them is finished.

Do you see one little pansy lifting its face to heaven, alone, but not insignificant? Nothing is too small to be seen by God.

Stop! And see! Does not this bring joy and beauty? Joys of many colors and fragrances? Stop! Be still and know the Creator of all. Do not disregard the lowly pansy. The Lord knows which flower shall drop her seed among you.

Worthy Art Thou

Create in me now a clean heart
Let me never from Thy way depart
Put a song in my heart and joy as I go
Hold me fast and I'll not be brought low

Put Your spirit within
My strength renew
Help me tell forth
Thy praises in all I do

For the joy of Your presence
Glad songs I will raise
Open my mouth, Lord
Thou art worthy of praise

Teach me Thy wisdom
In my secret heart
Renew me each day
That I shall not depart

Take not Thy Holy Spirit
Even a little bit away
But fill me anew
With each passing day

Thou art my strength, my sword and my shield
O Blessed Master, renew me at heart
That Thy worthy praises
I may to others impart

Psalm 51

Paul's Letter to Timothy

God has not given us a spirit of fear, but a sound mind,
full of power and love so pure.
So be not ashamed of the testimony of our Lord,
but gladly take affliction, His word is your sword.

He has saved and called you with a holy call,
and not according to our works, His grace is free to all.

Be strong in the faith that is in Christ our Lord,
endure this hardness gladly as His soldier adored.

If a man would strive for masteries, yet he is not crowned,
except he strive lawfully, he will not in grace abound.

For if we should own the world, what is there to gain?
But if we suffer for Him, we shall also reign.

The servant of the Lord must not strive, but be gentle unto all,
and follow after righteousness and listen for His call.

In and out of season, preach His holy Word, rebuke, reprove, exhort
That man may recover himself from the snare of Satan's court.

If I Could Tell You

Dear friend, I don't know what to say
Should I just look the other way
Not interfere, or burden anyone?
Seems there's nothing to be said or done

But maybe a smile or a hand on your arm
Is something I can do that won't cause harm
Would just my presence tell you that I care
And somehow in your pain, could it ease your share?

Dear friend, I want to be near to comfort you
To be the hands and heart of Jesus in all that He would do
For He has no hands but mine in this world today
And He would use His children in His will and way

Praise Him

Praise the Lord! Praise the Lord forever!
The wonders of His love, hell shall not sever
When trials come, I shall stand
For I know that He still holds my hand

Praise the Lord! Praise the Lord, my soul!
To touch His garment would make me whole
I'll be not shaken as a reed
For He knows my every need

Praise the Lord! The Living Tree
Whose root of life flows through me
So in His love I'll rise and sing
I am a recipient of the Holy King!

Five Minutes' Time

When I look into a star-filled night
Five minutes' time I see without number
With the lightning's flash and the thunder's might
How small I am

Electric currents, three thousand times around our planet
In five minutes' time,
Who could plan it?
How small I am

Revolves six thousand miles this earth in orbit
Five minutes of time
Who can absorb it?
How small I am

Fifty-five million miles travels a ray of light
In five minutes
It reaches me, shining bright
How small I am

Of the depths of the ocean, who can explore it?
Five minutes of time
In a cyclone, who could ignore it?
How small I am

God hears each word that I have said
Five minutes of time, how small I am
He cares for each tear that I have shed
How blessed I am

Hands

Beautiful hands all knotted and worn
      They have toiled for me since I was born
From a hard rebuke, to a soft caress
      Or folded in reverent prayerfulness

Beautiful hands so tired and still
      Now his own needs he cannot fill
Others must come to carry on
      For all the strength of these are gone

Dear God, may I give Thee mine
      To be used in all Thy ways divine
I will serve as these have done
      Until at last my victory is won

Feet of the Hinds

I'm pressing towards the summit like a determined mountaineer
    Where the clouds are left behind, and the air is serene and clear
At times the way is rugged, with boulders in the way
    Then the One who gently leads me, bids me rest and pray

The light again is breaking and I see the way to go
    But why should I press on when the going is so slow?
O that summit is so glorious, and I shall at last be free
    To rise above my troubles and more clearly see

For Jesus is my Leader and He's already there
    And He goes before, and for me He does prepare
He gives me feet of hinds when the crevice is wide and deep
    And prepares for me a refuge where I may rest and sleep

When the mountain towers before me and there seems no way to go
    I do not look upon the mountain, but upon the One Who loves me so
For His love will never lead me where I should not be
    so I press on towards life's summit, His blessed face to see

Salt of the Earth

Pride comes before a fall
Am I not the Giver of it all?
My Word is always fresh and sweet
I'll give you the words to repeat

Let your treasures be a few
Have I not said I'd care for you?
You must return to your first Love
To keep your blessing from above

What is man that he should boast?
Except in the power of the Holy Ghost?
I am the Giver of life and breath
Warn my people: Sin is death!

If you will use your voice for Me
I will bless your spirit abundantly
Keep your eyes on me, My son
I am the Lord, the Holy One

Christian Cocoons

I am but a small cocoon securely fastened on this branch
　　　And I am much too small, to leave my pew and take a chance
If I just stay hidden here, I won't become defiled
　　　Lord, You know all around me everything is wild
I have peeped a time or two and found the air was sweet
　　　Here I am safe and comfortable, yet am I complete?
Something now has happened, I no longer am satisfied
　　　Am I in captivity, with nothing left inside?
I will go out and try my wings, though it does scare me
　　　But I must venture farther out to find Your plan I see
Milk no longer satisfies, and I must have the meat
　　　Lord, I will do as You say. I am in You complete
Outside my safe cocoon is not the easy road
　　　But Your light and power are so much more than my own abode
My wings become stronger and I feel so free
　　　Praise You, precious Jesus. It's not myself, but Thee!

Thistle Flower

Let us not become a withered flower in the Lord's bouquet
But let us blossom gently, with faces turned His way
Also let your perfume sweetly scent the air
That others may see these blossoms, in God's garden fair

Reflecting the love of Jesus freely, as they pass
Though I be no more than a thistle flower peeping through the grass
For the Lord is where you look for Him, in the high place and the low
And anyone who seeks will find, if we His love will show

Consolation

I am brought low that I might be lifted
As the sands of the shore, I must be sifted
When the roaring tide moves in and out
With all its splendor it brings in doubt

Though the breakers seem to wash me clean
They leave what before I had not seen
I need to go in the valley deep
Lest I sit in my splendor half asleep

Though I may long for the coming tide
I know from God I cannot hide
Where I am weak He makes me strong
And keeps me when I would go wrong

Lord, forgive those who would lead me astray
And use them instead to strengthen my way
If I gained the world but lost my soul
How could You then my heart console?

I must be strong to stand the test
So for the Lord, I may do my best
Without the low, there is no high
thanks be to God! He is always nigh

Lost

I saw a little child, lost and alone
On an empty beach where the sun had shone
With the evening shadows coming on
Life's securities seemed all gone

She clutched a rag doll in her hand
Love was all she could understand
Is there anyone to care?
To hear as she cried out in despair?

The waves are raging, the beach is cold
Does anyone care, this child to hold?
Jesus said to seek the lost while He may be found
For truly the harvest does abound

Would you bring a child to heaven's gate?
Do not wait to hear, 'Too late, too late!'
It's not a command to Christians everywhere
God is love, and you must care

For across the waves the words are ringing
And I can hear the angels singing
Jesus pleads, 'Bring the lost ones unto Me
For I am coming soon, to ransom thee'

God's Children

Bless Your people, Lord
Give them love and grace
To do Thy work, O Lord
'Til we behold Thy face

Touch Your people, Lord
May they Your holy Presence feel
Till they know Your works, O Lord
And at Thy cross will kneel

Sanctify Your people, Lord
Oh, keep them ever true
And give them words, O Lord
To speak Your truths anew

Anoint Your people, Lord
With Thy holy Oil
And make us worthy, Lord
To in Thy vineyard toil

Give Thanks

Give thanks to the Lord
For Jesus Christ
He gave His life
He paid the price
To set me free
Of all my sin
That Your Holy Spirit
May dwell within
Thank you, Lord
for this blessed country
Into your bounty
You gave us the key
We are so blessed
By Your mighty hand
May we give You honor
In this great land
Put on us
Your garment of peace
That all over this world
Your light shall increase
Thank you, Lord, for food to eat
thanks for cold; thanks for heat
thanks for rain; thanks for snow
You planned it all, this I know
Nothing is worthy
To stand in Your place
You have made us sons
To walk in Your grace
You are the one true God
Creator of all
Our Father in Heaven
On You I call
I look unto Thee
And truly say
Whatever, Lord
Should come my way
I will give it now
Unto Thee
You are gracious and holy
And You love even me

God's Child

My child, My child, I know your state
Just step on through My open gate
If you feel Satan has you bound
Remember he flees when My Spirit's around

The gate before you is open wide
So step out in faith and come inside
You'll find my love is sweet and warm
And you'll be safe from evil and harm

I shall forgive your every sin
Believe, My child, and step right in
Within these gates, you will find rest
For you are numbered with the blest

Prayer

Holy Spirit, dwell within!
My flesh is weak and bound by sin
I need Thy help to talk to God
Rule me with Thy righteous rod

I humbly seek a closer walk
Keep me true though some would mock
I shall not fear though my life they take
But fear the one who my spirit would break

Dear Lord, I am my brother's keeper
My love for him must grow much deeper
In Thy love, Lord help me grow
So Thy mercy I may show

To all I meet I'm as a book
Clean the pages as they look
I pray they will get a glimpse of Thee
And Your great love for humanity

Keep me ready to do Thy will
That what You ask I will fulfill
I am no more than a speck of dust
But that speck could move men's hearts to trust

Holy Spirit, stay with me forever!
I would have no life if the lines would sever
Thy bounteous blessings I do not deserve
But I am Thy servant, willing to serve

Send Your Spirit

Send Your Spirit upon me, Lord
To bring good tidings to the meek
Help me light the way to righteousness
For there are those who seek
Lord, send Your anointing upon me
To bind the heart that's broken
And to set the captives free

Send Your love upon me, O Lord
To comfort those those who mourn
And keep me in Your wisdom
To deliver those unborn
Help me be Your servant
To open the prison gate
And loose the bonds of wickedness
Before it is too late

Send Your power upon me, Lord
Thy coming to proclaim
To warn me of Thy judgment
On all who reject Your Name
Send Your Spirit upon me, Lord
Make me wholly Thine
Cleanse within this vessel
That Your light through me may shine

Fill me with Your Spirit
That I may do all things
For nothing can withstand
What Your Holy Spirit brings
Then as Your Spirit dwells within
My lamp is full of oil
And I'll have Your light

My Book

Is my cover pliable or hard
       Do I keep my inner self on guard
Does my cover become my crust
       Or is it too soft for some to trust

Lord open up my every page
       It matters not its form or age
May others see all things anew
       Open their eyes to see only You

For You are the author of my book
       No matter how my pages look
May they see beyond my tattered scroll
       To find the lover of their soul

I may be the only book they can read
       So I seek Your word to fill our need
I need Your light so all may see
       The Holy Spirit abides in me

I was born in Wisconsin on a small farm, and I was one of nine children. We lived during the end of the Depression so we knew some very hard times. But I am so thankful for my Christian heritage because I always knew God was alive.

I started writing poetry in my early teens and believe the Lord answers prayer even through poems from the heart and pen. When troubles seem to mount up, I always feel a need to write. The Lord speaks through Psalms and countless ways if we but listen. My prayer is to pass these poems on to you, that they will also speak to you. I pray the Lord will direct your path wherever you are in life.

I am no longer young, but I am young at heart because the Lord has made it so. Now for all who read this book, please know the Lord truly does love you, and so do I.

Dee Hansen Alcorn

www.ingramcontent.com/pod-product-compliance
Lightning Source LLC
Chambersburg PA
CBHW041425090426
42741CB00002B/31